Small Hand, Big Money

Journey To Financial Freedom

Dong Doan

© Copyright 2021 by - All rights reserved. This document is geared towards providing exact and reliable information in regards to the topic and issue covered. The publication is sold with the idea that the publisher is not required to render accounting, officially permitted, or otherwise, qualified services. If advice is necessary, legal or professional, a practiced individual in the profession should be ordered from a Declaration of Principles which was accepted and approved equally by a Committee of the American Bar Association and a Committee of Publishers and Associations. In no way is it legal to reproduce, duplicate, or transmit any part of this document in either electronic means or in printed format. Recording of this publication is strictly prohibited and any storage of this document is not allowed unless with written permission from the publisher. All rights re- served. The information provided herein is stated to be truthful and consistent, in that any liability, in terms of inattention or otherwise, by any usage or abuse of any policies, processes, or directions contained within is the solitary and utter responsibility of the recipient reader. Under no circumstances will any legal responsibility or blame be held against the publisher for any reparation, damages, or monetary loss due to the information here- in, either directly or indirectly. Respective authors own all copyrights not held by the publisher. The information herein is offered for informational purposes solely and is universal as so. The presentation of the information is without a contract or any type of guarantee assurance. The trademarks that are used are without any consent, and the publication of the trademark is without permission or backing by the trademark owner. All trademarks and brands within this book are for clarifying purposes only and are owned by the owners them- selves, not affiliated with this document

Table Of Contents:

Introduction

Chapter 1 : Decision Making

Chapter 2: 7 Rules Of Money You Will Not Learn In School

Chapter 3: 5 Money Secrets I Wish I Learned In School

Chapter 4: The Reason Why You Will Not Get Out Of Debt

Chapter 5: Creating Your Life Goals

Chapter 6: Creating Your Financial Game Plan

Chapter 7: Creating My Personal Wealth

Chapter 8: Finding Extra Income

Chapter 9: How To Invest Money

Chapter 10: Money Scammers And Protecting Your Asset

Chapter 11: Enjoy Your Money

Conclusion

Introduction

Do you remember when you were smaller how small your hand was and how big a quarter was in your hand or how big a dollar was? Now that you are bigger, your hand grew, but money slips out your hand like you are still a little kid. It is time for that to stop!

Quick story of my life; I am a first-generation Vietnamese American where my family did not have much financial literacy, and the only thing I knew growing up is that money comes and goes, and you should enjoy it now. I have spent money as fast as I could get it so that no one else in my family could spend it for me, and that was because of what my parents, family, and friends did around me even though at the age of 15 I had my first job as a lifeguard for the summer and the following month I also found a job at a restaurant washing dishes. I was bringing about 1- 2 thousand a week at the age of 15, and by the age of 16, I had three jobs and never had a day off work. That I had 2 or 3 jobs does not mean I had the money; I just knew how to work for money. With all my time working, I wouldn't have time to spend money or learned how to handle money. That was not the case; no one was teaching me how to handle money; all I saw was an advertisement everywhere and I do go for the newest and greatest thing that comes out, and I had to have it.

I remember every day waking up at 6:00 am so that I could walk to the pool from my house so that I could be there on time to start my job so that I could be done by 11:00 am. I would then walk home so that I could go take a nap and go back to my second job at the restaurant, and that would take the rest of my day until midnight. I returned home from work, and my dad was sitting there, drinking his beer, and told me to sit down with him. He then informs me he cannot afford to send me to college and only think he can afford to send one of his three kids to college, and he would then go into stating that you are not smart enough to go to college. No one told me there were other methods to go to college like a student loan, grants, or financial aid. We just did not talk about much in my family or friend group. I did not know where to start at that time to even look up the information.

There is no reason to blame my father for this situation because my grade was awfully bad for a typically Asian American. My lack of interest in the education system is a big factor in why my father did not want to spend money on his son. My parents never had their focus on their children's education. Well, the first two children in the family were more of a workforce, just to help with earning money. From working on a shrimp boat at the age of 6 to waking up at 3 am every day to help my mother throw newspaper so that my parents could pay bills and buy a thing to keep up with the Jones. To think back to it, my family was the Jones of the community, and no one knew what we had to go through to get those items to show off to everyone.

Knowing that I needed to do something that could send me to college, I had decided to join the military due to the fact my father informing me, they could not afford to send me to college and only had enough to send one kid to college, and it was not me so instead of bothering my parents I decided to join the military at the age of 17 so that I could get an education for myself. At that time, no one informed me how college works or how it gets paid for. My parents just informed me that they could not afford to send me to one and no one around me knew anything about the college system, about free grants and loans.

Now that I think about it, I was not a bad child or an uneducated kid. I had a bad representation in school, not sure why, but that's in the past. I was away, just tired of working with my parents all afternoon after school. Never pushed to my limit on education or got the attention from my parents to do so as a certain family event happens during the time I was growing up that their attention could not be on me, but the older child had to get the attention due to some incident that causes him to get kicked out school. My parents had to turn their attention to their old child and not ignore me but pay less attention to my education. I was able to graduate early at the age of 17 so that I could ship off to the military.

My parents were so focused on making money to pay for a thing they used to show off, all I did was work and never even study a day in my life. I didn't make the bad grade, but it wasn't all A's; it was a mix of A's, B's, and a C' or 2 in the mix. Instead of hitting the books, I was working with my mother at the factory heading shrimp, working on the boats for shrimping, cleaning fish so she could sell it to the market to make money. I still got to do some school activities, so it wasn't like child labor; it was just any extra time used around working to make more money.

When I went to the military, it was one of the best times of my life. It was a very life-changing event. I got to see all the different views of the world. I fell for a lot of the same trick everyone else did while in the military. Spending every penny, I made in the military on the thing I could not afford, such as cars, motorcycles, news electronic, and mostly partying. Thinking I finally made it and coming home on vacation one time, I got to see my older brothers' paycheck, and it wasn't much, but it was more than double of mine. I was shocked here I was serving in the military, an E-2 making less than a gas station worker.

After some time, I started to make rank and was able to make E-5 in 4 years with the grind and studying to make it. I was happy for myself, and finally. However, I made it, but then one of my E-7 sat down with me and told me, "Since you been under my wing, I see that you are too smart to stay in the military it is only going to hold you back financially, and if you wanted a family, it does not exist in the military". He was a 32-year-old man going through a divorce, I see why he was telling me all these. He lost everything while we were deployed to the middle east: his family, friends, and money all gone to his spouse.

Chapter One

Making A Decision

I decided to get out of the military and make something more of myself. This was the turning point I could say that change my life. I still did not know how to handle my money, but now I was 22-year-old and had more ambition to prove that I could make it in life. At that time, I did not know what I was going to do, but I knew that I did not want to work for the rest of my life. Here is where I started my financial journey of the unspoken rules of money, with which a simple search on the internet, you can find out any information you want.

"The only person that would know what will make you happy is you"

Deciding to get out and get my education was the automatic answer I got on how to make more money than the average person. At that time, all I wanted was to be better than the average person and not live paycheck to paycheck. No one has taught me financially in my 22 years of life, and the only thing I knew was how to work. The only person that would know what will make you happy is you. It could be retiring at the age of 30 so that you can enjoy the rest of your life or it just to get a better job for yourself to support your family. Friends, family, and co-worker was telling me I was an idiot for leaving the comfort of the military a guaranteed job with good retirement at the age of 37-year-old (join the military at age 17). My commanding officer was informing me that I had a great future ahead of me if I stayed in the military. I did not have to worry about making ranking anymore because I had made the minimum requirement to allow me to do 20 years. My father told me in a car ride during my leave home from the military, he said; "if you do not get out, you will never do anything with your life. You won't find a job and you're not smart enough to go to college". He gave me an example of one of his friend's son that got out of the military and just stayed at home to play video games, without knowing what I know now. My father never believes in anything in me until I prove him wrong. I do not know why he never believes in me, but if I were not mentally stronger from the military, that could have caused me to fail. Thank you, United States Navy; you help set my life in the right direction.

It is time for you to decide how you want to live your life as I did not want to waste any more time in the military, making a penny for what I was doing. I had decided to go to college and get an education to make more money, and it was the only thing I knew at the time on how to guarantee my income to be better than the average person. Do not let anyone tell you that you can't do anything in your life. It is better to try and fail than not try at all. As you read here, I did not have my family support mentally or financially, and I still got to where I am at today.

Did I make a good investment into going to college for an engineering degree that I did not use? I believed that since the military paid for school, it was one of the best investments I made for myself. I might not be using my education to its fullest that I can use it for, but I learn a lot more than what was just in the book. I got to meet more people and build my network of professional people. That was when I started to wake up to how to build wealth. I had to watch a professional engineer making 200k a year living paycheck to paycheck go bankrupt five years from retirement, but an engineering tech making 80k a year living off less than he made, he was able to retire a millionaire. His informations started to teach me all these financial rules and secrets that you need to be financially successful; the first thing he taught me was to invest in yourself first for the biggest return. He spent a few thousand to get his certification to become an engineering tech, and with just that, he was able to retire a millionaire.

"Do not let anyone tell you that you can't do anything in your life. It is better to try and fail than not try at all"

Go out and invest the money into yourself; it does not matter what it is if you think it will improve your life. The best return anyone ever can make it into oneself. If you cannot do public speaking, go take some public speaking classes; those classes might give you a better opportunity in the future in an interview, speaking in a meeting, or even doing a presentation for your company. That one investment might give you a raise in your current job or future career.

Invest in oneself is the best decision anyone can ever make, and everyone should go out and try to improve themselves to be a better version of themselves the next day. If you want other people's opinions to change, you should change how you think of yourself. I spoke to plenty of professional engineers that away doubt their skill and knowledge, instead of going out and trying to improve their skill, they just take it as I am not good at a certain skill. Then they wonder why they get passed upon promotion or not get there raised that they believed they deserved. If you do not want to be overlooked, keep polishing your skill to stay on top of your industry.

"Invest in oneself is the best decision anyone can ever make, and everyone"

I help many people get what they want next in their life by giving them this advice. Pushing them to do a thing to help improve themselves, maybe that is what your calling is. To improve your life to help others to improve theirs.

You will not take advice from a bum on the street, so why would you ask just anyone, or why would anyone ask you for advice if you are not worth listening to. You need to find someone worth listening to and not waste your time on fake people or people who act like their situation is better than yours. If you want to get wealthy, go find someone that is wealthy and ask them how they did it. We live in the digital age; you can google and YouTube everything now to find the help you need to improve yourself. You can be raised poor, but it is your fault if you do not improve your life.

Deciding on what you want in the future is the first phase of knowledge on how to get there. If you write down, I want to be a millionaire; then you need to write down how you are going to get there and how you are going to do it. I know tons of people that tell me I want to be rich, but I ask what is rich? Do you know what the difference between being poor and broke is? Also, what is the difference between being rich and wealthy?

What is the definition of being poor? It is lack of sufficient money to live at a standard considered comfortable or normal in a society? Now let us compare that to the definition of being broke as "having to completely run out of money for the moment you are in". If you are poor, you put yourself in and set the mood that you are always going to be like that. You can break and get out of the situation you are in. Do not set your mood in a situation where you can't get out; you are not poor; you are broke and will get out of it. Stop setting yourself in a situation you cannot get out of. Tell yourself I am just broke right now and will be out of this eventually.

When I was a young boy, I thought that being rich and wealthy was the same thing, but there is a difference between them. Rich may mean you have a lot of cash; you may also have a lot of expenses that keep you up at night, such as your mortgage, private school tuitions, and more. In short, if you are rich, you are often trying to keep up with the rat race.

I have come across many definitions of the word wealth in my research on financial education. The best way to define wealth is through an equation. How many days will you survive, financially speaking, if you quit working today? How long would you be able to live with the sum of money you have?

"Wealth is a measure in time, not dollars"

It is that simple:

For example, if your monthly expenses are $4,000 and you have a saving of $40,000, your wealth is approximately ten months or about 300 days. But if you are expenses are $4,000, and you have investments that provide $4,000 a month, you are infinitely wealthy.

Wealth is a measure in time, not dollars. This problem of wealthy vs. wealthy or poor vs. broke a significant one because poor mindsets are often revealed. If you can't stop working and bust your ass to buy liability after liability to keep up with the rat race or the Jones, being rich means nothing.

Do you want to be rich or wealthy? Follow these rules of money, and you will be well on your way to becoming wealthy.

Chapter Two

7 Rules Of Money You Will Not Learn In School

Most people treat talking about money and wealth management as a taboo. No one talks about how they earn money or how much debt they are in. For years, I used these rules to get out of a weird situation, to make the most of my time, and get an edge over other people. I used to be a slave to money, and after I follow these seven rules, I became a master of money.

Rule number 1: "Anyone can be wealthy; you just need to apply yourself"

Wealth creation is a skill that is learned, implemented, and practiced. Knowing that you have the same right and opportunities as anyone else, make as much as you want from it. You must find a way to make money; sitting there every afternoon watching Netflix for 2-4 hours a day is time wasted; you could have been working on a side job to get out of debt, save for retirement, or even get ahead of your peer. Use your free time in life to improve yourself with skills that you can earn more money. The key is, the more you learn, the more you earn. Make yourself worth something so that you can create more money in the future.

"Use your free time in life to improve yourself with skills that you can earn more money, the key is, the more you learn, the more you earn"

To find a career that you desire, see what the job requirement you need is then go get it. If you want to be a graphic designer, spend 5 min and type in google. What is the job requirement to become a graphic designer? There will be plenty of results showing you how to become a graphic designer? If you are in a career, you might enjoy going to your boss or employer and asking them what the requirement is to advance your career. If they don't answer, that is not a work environment you want to stay in. If you are a waiter, go to the owner of the restaurant and tell them, "I love this job and working for you. How can I become a manager?" and they tell you there no room to improve, then you need to find a place that will.

If you don't want to work for anyone, find a side job you can do with your current job until it takes off. If you are a hairstylist and one day you want to open your hair salon, you can plait hair and build your client lists now. Don't stop working at your current employer until your side income can support your current living. This step could take you one week or even 5-year time; it all depends on how much effort you put into the side business. There is a way to find a side job that you could do with your current schedule. If you have a skill or knowledge that someone else doesn't know, use that to find your side income. Help your future self. Don't expect others to help you.

Rule number two: **"Spend Less Than You Earn"**

The simplest of concepts and yet something everyone continuously failed at for a very long time. If you want to continue to have money in the bank, you need to spend less than you earn. Before you spend your money, think to yourself, this item costs me x amount of hour to work to determine if you want the item. If it cost you 20 hours to work so that you can have fun in one night of going out with your friends, is it worth those 20 hours of work? That is half of the week's pay just to have fun for a few hours. The worst thing I hear from people is, " I always can make more money later" yes, this is true; you can away make more money later until it is too late. This isn't just coming from young people; this is also coming from people a few years from retirement. Create a simple budget that you can live by, and just don't create a budget; follow up with the budget with your expenses report from what you spent.

The best way to create a budget is to get your last three months of expense from your bank and put it into an excel sheet or word document and categorize all your expenses out and see what you spend your money on. It doesn't make sense to create a budget without knowing what you need money for. It is like buying a light bulb for a car and not know which light bulb you are needing. Sit down and look at what you need the money for and create your budget, see where you can lower some of your expenses. Live within your means, your savings is the key to your success. Money not seen is money not missed.

Rule Number 3: "Money will only solve the money problem, nothing more, nothing less"

Money doesn't change people. If the person is greedy before he had money, he will be greedy when he has money. If the person is a jerk with money, he will still be a jerk without money. People don't change very easily. They stick to how they naturally are. I always taught money is bad and causes people to be evil but when I was starting to grow my wealth, I found out it was false.

What happened to me when I started to grow my wealth. I started to give back to the community more; it didn't make me evil; it made me become more giving. I donated a large number of my earnings back to the community in all different forms. Still, you never hear about it because it is not newsworthy, but when you hear a scandal on a rapper, professional athlete, or a billionaire/millionaire spending the money they earn to buy themselves a million-dollar house, it makes them evil. Still, they donated 2 million to families in need.

Don't listen to an outsider on how you should spend your money. The only person that should tell you how to spend your hard-earned money is you. If it doesn't hurt or damage anyone else life, then you shouldn't have any problem in your future when you start building wealth. Your wealth building is done by you and should be spent how you want to spend it.

Rule Number 4: "Do not chase money; instead, let money chase you"

I chased money for years; for me getting rich was the American dream. Most people I knew wanted to be rich, but few of them made it a priority. It's a glorious idea but chasing money for the sake of money is a sure way to end up with nowhere. Getting rich is hard, and there is no shortcut to success, you must work your ass off. You must give yourself over to something completely. You must build something so valuable that people are willing to trade their hard-earn money, and that requires blood, sweat, and tears.

A lot of people have incredible noble goals. They see problems in the world and envision a solution. They dream of helping others and providing service for a generation to come. Without a vision, your goals will be much more difficult to reach. Still, some are an indispensable factor for succeeding; one of the most is having the vision to do something.

With a sense of purpose, you will work harder because you know there are motivation and reward at the end of the tunnel. Do what you love, and the money will eventually come? That isn't away from the case, but you can be wealthy doing what you love. You might not be the richest person in the world, but you will be happy to go to work and give better results as a result of that. The more valuable you become, the more valuable you are.

"Investing your money is like sending your army out to bring back the spoil of war"

I made money chase me by not worrying about money. I stopped thinking about the money itself and instead focused on creating value for myself and others. I realized that sounds like a cliché as it sounds. So, get out there and stop chasing money. Do it long enough, and the money will chase you. Don't be a slave to money; become the master of money.

Rule number 5: "Money does not grow on a tree unless you plant the seed"

It takes time for a tree to mature from a small seed to a fully grown tree: It could take a decade or longer indeed. Eventually, it gets tall, solid, and produces many leaves. In reality, it will decide how well it can do in the future based on what you feed or how well the tree does.

Leaving your hard earned money in a savings account is causing your money to lose value. I am not saying you should put your life saving into an investment, but anything after your 3-6-month emergency fund should be invested until you become wealthy enough to live off your investment. Investing your money is like sending your army out to bring back the spoil of war. Some of them will come back with more money, and others will die in battle. It takes time to build up your army; it could be 5-year, seven-year, or even more. The sooner you start, the sooner you will earn more from the spoil of war that your money brings back.

Don't let people fool you with fast money. There are a few who end up wealthy overnight, but the chances that you will be the one isn't very high. If you just invest your time and money in a good long-term investment, you will end up wealthy overtime. Becoming rich overnight is chasing the money, and you will end up poor by the end of the road, just like how most people who win the lottery end up worst off than they started. Building the foundation of your wealth is one of the most important in wealth building.

Rule number 6: "Some people are rich, and there are wealthy people"

The difference between wealthy and rich people is that wealthy people do not worry about money, and the rich have a lot of money. Doctors and lawyers who may be in the sense of salaries are in the higher economic range, however because of their expenses houses, cars, student loan debt, private school tuition, practice overhead, sometimes poor decision, etc., makes them start their financial journey relatively later in life with much more debt. In the end, becoming rich has more to do with financial independence. Which means you're not living paycheck to paycheck. It means either you've invested enough that you don't need jobs every day to support your lifestyle, or you've built up enough residual, passive income to get paid in your sleep.

I don't care personally if I'm wealthy; I don't need a luxurious house or cars. I just want to know that if I want to spend time with my family without any financial burden, I can leave any or all work. I recall hearing, somewhere, "wealth is measured in time, not dollars" and I think that's real.

Being affluent only means making a lot of profits. It may also mean, investment and not money borrowing. It's not like it's wrong to be famous, it just means you are doing something wasteful unless you still create money.

Rule number 7: "The right partner can make you wealthy, and the wrong person can make you poor"

Getting married or moving in with your partner is a life-changing event; this will also include your finances. I am not saying that finding a wealthy partner or a poor partner should be a factor of being your partner, but their habit should be taking into account on who you should pick. It doesn't have to be daunting to learn to jointly manage your assets. As long as you put in the effort, it is something every couple can do.

Get underway on a journey for you and your wife to a rich future by:

- Talking about money
- Write down goals
- Create a plan
- Save for a rainy day
- Tackle any lingering debt
- Saving for the future

Talking about your money, as uncomfortable as this may be, money in conversations are crucial, and the earlier you and your partner talk finances, the better. The number one reason why people have a divorce is money problem or money issue. You should not ever presume that both you and your family would be on the same page in any manner when it comes to how you organize your money and who is responsible for what. You want to start by knowing your partner's financial history, finding out his or her feelings towards money and what they consider to be its purpose in their life. This will allow you to understand how you both can make a financial decision together. It will allow both of you to understand your spending habits and set the mindset ahead of marriage instead of being blindsided after the honeymoon phase is over.

Write down the goal; the first step as a couple is to dream together. What are you and your spouse hunting for? It could be a holiday home, more wealth, or a trip together around the world. Make your targets clear, comprehensive, and complete. People who write down their goals get rich. It's a fact. Study after study shows that writing down your goal makes it much more likely you'll achieve them.

Create a plan; step one is to understand where you're starting from. Knowing what your net worth is and if either of you has any assets, liabilities, and expenses. Write them all on a piece of paper and figure out what step you should take to get to your future.

Save for a rainy day; things don't always don't go as planned. People lose their jobs, businesses don't do so well one year, and primary earners get sick. By establishing an emergency fund, you want to hope for the best but brace for the worst. How much emergency fund is depending on what strategy you go with to build your wealth. Most people would suggest a minimum of three months worth of expenses, but you need to decide together on what makes sense for the two of you.

Any loan credit card debt that is remaining will ruin the matrimony. It does not matter how much you love someone if you continuously invest in debt in a relationship, I can tell you now that you will eventually end the relationship. If it's your partner who accumulated mounds of debt, encourage him or her to work on erasing those balances for a debt they acquired before your marriage. After the marriage, it becomes a collective hindrance as your finances merge; knowing each other's credit score and financial situation is a need before marriage if you want a successful marriage. This doesn't mean you can't get married, but as long you both get on the same page on how you want to handle the debt, it creates a better marriage rate.

Saving the hope for the future is not for children alone. You and your partner should think high. What will you both do in the future? Every adult deserves to dream, but there is also a financial advantage to the dream. How will you get to where you want to be? Is it saving 50% of your income to retire early? Is it to pay for your kid's future? Decide your future and start working towards your goal by saving what needs to be set aside. It best to have everything especially a wealth-building program where you speak with a financial advisor or set a goal together and figure out a game plan.

Now that you know the seven rules of money. You need to learn the secrets of money that they do not teach you in school either. I used both this information to help me get out of the rat race and put me in the wealthy category that few people ever received after I got into this level of freedom of not needing to live paycheck to paycheck and it created a different outlook at work.

Chapter Three

5 Money Secretes I Wished I Learned In School

I love the thought of acquiring new talent, developing and being a better person, but there is something about school that brings a certain sense to education, such as a form of restriction. Don't get me wrong, I'm an educational champion, but when you quit your 12 years of school, there is a relaxed feeling, and you don't know what a credit is or how to even build a budget for your monthly expenses. I believe in lifelong learning. That one must continue acquiring new knowledge, developing oneself, and expanding horizons. It is important you take note of the following:

> *"People who can delay gratification and sacrifice immediate wants for the long-term benefit are the ones who build real wealth"*

1. Delaying gratification can change your financial future.

2. You are on your own financially; no one will come and save you.

3. Passive revenue is much more significant than active revenue.

4. Money Mindset.

5. Assets put money in your wallet; liabilities pull money out of your pocket.

Delaying gratification can change your financial future

Personal finance is much more about behavior and mindset than money and math. It takes self-awareness and discipline to walk into a store and only purchase the one item we went in there for. We are not rational when it comes to money, and we must understand ourselves well enough to contract it. The principle of delayed gratification is very important to be savvy with money. We now live in a world we can have anything within 24 hours, but real wealth is still a slow, methodical process. Even though we can pay for everything on a credit card, it is best to wait and pay cash. People who can delay gratification and sacrifice immediate wants for the long-term benefit are the ones who build real wealth. Studies suggest that delayed fulfillment is one of good people's most effective personal characteristics. People who learn to handle their needs at this time are more prosperous than people who give in to their jobs, marriages, fitness, and finances. Being able to delay satisfaction isn't the easiest skill to acquire, it involves feeling dissatisfied, which is why it seems impossible for people who haven't learned to control their impulses. Choosing to have something now might feel good but making an effort to have discipline and manage your impulses can result in bigger or better rewards in the future. Over time, delaying gratification will improve your self-control and ultimately help you achieve your long-term goals faster.

You are on your own financially

If you are close to retirement and have nothing saved for retirement, no one is going to come to save your hand, your money. Social security is not guaranteed, and your employer won't support you for the next phase of your life. There very few people who get a pension plan, which is a basic financial arrangement with a company to fund your retirement as a percentage of your salary in exchange for many years of working at the company. Don't assume you will be able to work until you die. Your health can prevent you from working at the age of 40, can get in an accident, or even force retirement from your current employer. Don't wait until it is too late to start saving up for retirement. Following Experian, in 2020, only one-fourth of Americans don't have any retirement savings. A survey performed by the Transamerica Workforce Studies Center reveals that 64 percent of seniors did not get support from their employers when moving to retirement. 41% said that they expect that their investments will make them a holiday home, and a little more than a third said that in their golden years, they want to spend their time with loved ones and that the world will follow them. However, according to a survey conducted by GOBankingRate, more than half of Americans have under $1000 on their savings account.

Passive revenue is much more significant than active revenue

There is only two ways to make an income, and that is active income and passive income. There are a couple of ways you can earn an active income- that is, getting paid after you finish a job. You don't get paid unless you do something for a customer or an employer. If you are like me, that active income idea is good, but they aren't your only way of making money. Passive income is required to gain income during the initial effort. After you build the initial product, you do nothing more practically.

With the passive income, the money keeps growing even when you are sleeping, take a vacation, or even being sick. Much of your career experience is good; only from your 9-5 job and few side hustles can you gain active money. Although it does happen that (a) you no longer want to work to survive (b) because of sickness or accident, you are physically unable to function. You ought to consider searching for opportunities to earn it if you do not earn passive income. Possibly when you work and make immediate transfers, active income is easier to receive. It will take months or years to reach stable sources of income from passive income. And it will take you decades to swap your monthly wage for your monthly passive income.

There are different levels of passive income, and they will all have different risks, liquidity, income potential, upfront work, and maintenance work. Here are some of the different ways and challenges you will face if you choose one of these.

Real estate rental: The demand for real estate is immense. But the rental market is likely confined to single-family houses, condos, and multi-family homes for smaller investors. The purchasing of an apartment requires a lot of early effort. You conduct a lot of land analysis, you study the neighborhood, speak with lenders, if required, make fixes, carry out a land inspection, find a Superintendent of Assets (especially if it is an out-of-state property), check for tenants (and negotiate with them).

Real estate crowdfunding: Real estate crowdfunding helps small investors, run by experienced private equity operators, to buy into bigger real estate ventures. Exposure to multi-family homes, single-family housing, or even commercial land may be gained.

Dividend Income: One of the purest types of passive revenue is dividend income. The great thing about dividend investing is that it is very liquid and extremely tax-advantaged. Investing in dividends requires you to research stocks to keep up with data flow, including company earnings follow-up, conference calls, and other activities. Overall, I would suggest the best thing about investing in dividends is the opportunity for profits. Every single year, fantastic firms will pay and raise dividend payments, which means your predictable dividend checks can increase too!

eBooks: There is some upfront work needed for eBooks. It could take a lot of work, depending on what you write about. Non-fiction books, in general, need a lot more effort than fiction books.

Website/blog/niche platform: Of all the passive income sources I have mentioned, a niche site, blog, or website has the greatest earnings potential. They still need a lot of effort, though. Final thoughts for my three best sources of passive income are rental property, dividend income, and eBook.

Money Mindset

The sum of the attitudes and thoughts you carry to a situation relating to your finances is your money mentality. They are the mental patterns that you have to think about and react to every financial situation; your previous financial experiences typically generate them. What makes one person successful financially and another one gives up? The importance of understanding your money mindset. If you believe you can or cannot do something that will affect the overall result of what you are trying to do with your life, it becomes the sum of your experiences around money for better or worse.

- Successes and failures with money, yours or family and friends
- How our parents and wider family managed and dealt with money
- How our friends and frenemies talked and acted around money

• The books, magazines, tv, internet, and ideas around money that we actively or passively exposed ourselves to over the years.

All of these are also, of course, ongoing today, again actively or passively. We can choose to concentrate or expose ourselves to more positive mindsets or not as the mood takes us. How do you think about money? Do you see money as the end or merely the means to an end? Is it the price or just a tool to reach your prize?

What type of money mindset are you from below?

Poor Mindset

- Believe the government will support them
- Money avoider
- Spend everything they earn
- Live paycheck to paycheck
- They still say they don't have time, but they waste much of their time watching TV

Middle-Class Mindset

- Believe in good education
- Money worshiper
- Money status
- Have a high paying job
- Are saving for retirement
- Work for money

Wealthy Mindset

• Are entrepreneurs' mindset

• Money vigilant

• Thinking on ways to work more intelligently, not harder,

• Have capital that works for them

Below are some mindset practice that will help you change and strengthen your financial mindset:

• **Change your mindset/strengthen your mindset:** Read books that will positively influence your mind.

• **Understand that your mindset is like a muscle; it can be trained:** Think about your life up until now and ask yourself how you can change it. When faced with such obstacles, focus on your normal approach, what causes you to transition into a fixed mentality, and how do you return to a place of growth? Do you think that you are not 'strong enough' or question the ability to find a solution to a dilemma that you don't believe you have the ability to solve? Do you feel stressed and fear defeat, so concentrate your focus on other responsibilities and duties you know you are good at? Can you feel your defenses go up when given feedback? What I'm trying to say here is that at the main 'cause' points, listening to the sound in your head and what it's telling you, you need to think about how you feel. When you do, whether you are to switch from a fixed to a development mentality in any positive way, you will be able to pick out the unhelpful self-limiting narratives running around in your brain, narratives that you will need to silence.

• **Choose tasks that can be accomplished:** Overcome your fear of failing or being dumb, forget whatever self-doubt you have, and spend your time and attention on certain things on your to-do list that you find to be tougher than others. Try to view and approach these with a creative mindset as you do. Yes, maybe you'll crash. Yet you will discover more about yourself in the process that you might not otherwise have done, and what you will do next time to guarantee that you do well in the future. You will easily expand your expertise with a change in attitude and practice embracing this mindset as you continue to tackle any new task with confidence and trust instead of avoidance and apprehension.

- **Do not compare yourself to anyone else:** Adjust the way you look and understand how you might learn from them, instead. This entity you think is threatening, or daunting may have strategic skills to help you make a breakthrough on one of your unfinished ventures, or maybe they just have a certain way of doing stuff, of finding answers to an issue you've never thought of before. Start changing your thoughts to remember that everyone you meet is a chance to experience more from a new viewpoint. That's something not to be intimidated by, it's something to welcome.

- **Understand that you are not going to master your new mindset overnight:** Note, as soon as we start doing it, we are never as successful as we can reasonably be at a given talent. Instead, it takes work and time to learn. So, stop putting so much pressure on yourself if you take on a new challenge or start learning a new talent. Instead, recognize that at the outset, you will face challenges. Choose everything you can't do today, the one thing you've always got a mental block over. Spend time putting it into effect. Do not think about not immediately being good at it or about anyone else being stronger. Only work on your own learning experience from there, beginning tiny and developing your skills bit by bit. Over time, you will start to see progress – this will reinforce your inclination and confidence when it comes to learning, meaning you are far more likely to continue that journey rather than bailing out at the first hurdle.

- **Do not give up and understand this will take time and effort:** Just think about all the abilities you might have under your belt. Your stuck mentality keeps you from improving those items that could have earlier gotten you that promotion or are so crucial to increasing your company. Don't make the argument that you "don't have enough time" to build them, or "that's someone else's job," carve out the time instead. The highest-achieving person in history appreciated this. Only look at Albert Einstein, who noted that "it is not that I'm so smart, it's just that I stay with problems longer" So, now is the time to change your way of thinking for the sake of your financial success, to block those destructive thoughts that swirl through your head, those thoughts that have the power to deprive you of the chance to develop new skills that might help protect your future.

- **Assets put money in your wallet; liabilities pull money out of your pocket.**

Assets put money in your wallet; liabilities pull money out of your pocket. Assets bring liquidity to your firm and lifts the wealth of your company, while liabilities lower the value and equity of your company. The better the financial stability of your company, the more your assets outweigh your liabilities. But you might be on the cusp of going out of business if you find yourself with more liabilities than cash.

Examples of assets are:

- Cash

- Investments

- Inventory

- Office equipment

- Machinery

- Real estate

- Company-owned vehicles

Examples of liabilities are:

- Bank debt

- Mortgage debt

- Money owed to suppliers (accounts payable)

- Wages owed

- Taxes owed

Assets are often grouped according to their liquidity or the pace of currency exchange of the commodity. As it can be used directly to cover a debt, the most liquid asset on the balance sheet is cash. Like a warehouse, an illiquid commodity is the opposite since the sale period (converting the property to cash) may take longer.

Present reserves are considered the most liquid assets. These investments will be converted to cash in less than a year and include cash, marketable securities, inventory, and receivable accounts. For your company, these assets produce income.

Non-liquid assets are classified together under the fixed asset grouping. Real estate, cars, and equipment are among others. Fixed assets are purchased by the corporation and add to the sales but are not consumed in the course of raising profits and are not kept for cash conversion. Fixed assets are concrete objects that normally require considerable cash investment and endure for a prolonged period.

Current vs. Long-Term Liabilities

Liabilities are also classified into two categories: existing and long-term liabilities, respectively. Present liabilities are those payable in the year to come, while long-term liabilities are due at least one year longer.

Usually, existing liabilities reflect money owed to the object itself. Also, long-term interest obligations due in the next year will be counted in the current liabilities. For starters, if you owe a 5-year payment contract on your car and you are in the first two months of owning it. You owe more on the vehicle than you can get out of it and it causes it to be a liability, but if you own a car outright and the value is $10,000, you have a depressing asset.

One of the most significant goals as a small business owner would be to balance the accounts. That means that to make smart decisions and determine your company's health, you need a sound understanding of assets and liabilities. It's easy to grasp assets and liabilities once the terms are established, and the financial results you've been producing will start to have more significance!

Now that you know the rules of money and the five money secrets of money, you need to know what are some of the reasons you can't get out of debt.

Chapter Four

The Reason You Will Not Get Out Of Debt

One day I went to work and saw one of my co-workers look very depressed, and I started to ask her what was wrong. She had informed me she does not know what she was doing; she is 37-year-old and lives at home with her mom with her two kids and her husband. I was shocked to see that she was old and still had to live with her mom. She then asked me, "how did you get where you are?" You have your own house, two cars, a good investment, two kids, my own company, and a good retirement plan. She then looked me in the eyes and said, "My family makes more than you, and I have the same thing you have, but how are you doing so well? Did your parents give you money?"

I started to ask her do you know how much debt you have, do you have a budget, do you have a time management plan, do you have an expense report, do you know how much money you are bringing in, and lastly, what is your debt to income ratio? To my surprise, after talking to her for 4 hours, she didn't know where half her money was going. I don't know her salary or what her husband was, but I believe a pharmacist, following Glassdoor makes $110,000-$130,000, and an engineer makes on average $91,000 according to Glassdoor.

Have you ever felt like you are not getting anywhere in your financial journey? You are not alone. According to a 2019 survey by CreditCards.com, 25% of Americans with debt say they will never be able to pay off all the money they owe. Here are some of the most common reasons people fall deep into debt and cannot get out of it if you are in this situation. Identifying the reasons why and how you have gotten into this situation will help create an effective strategy to conquer the root of your debt.

You do not know how much you owe

A recent U.S. News survey observation noted that 21% of poll respondents were not even sure if they were carrying credit card debt at all. As a result, people do not even have an idea how long it will take to pay off debt and do not realize how debt is preventing them from reaching certain financial goals, such as early retirement. You should not intend to handle your debt if you do not take the time to find out how much you owe. Starting by making a list of your debts and then picking one debt to pay off. We will be exploring ways to tackle debt in the next chapter.

You only pay minimum

Making minimum payments each month is a guaranteed way to be stuck in debt much longer than necessary. For example, according to a Bankrate credit card calculator, if you have a $10,000 balance on a credit card with a 21 percent annual percentage rate and making a minimum monthly payment of just 2 percent of the balance, it would take you more than 27 years to pay off what you owe. Plus, by the time you pay that off, the cumulative interest rates over that period will amount to more than double the balance.

"You should not intend to handle your debt if you do not take the time to find out how much you owe"

By actually raising your monthly contribution to 3% of the balance rather than 2%, you will nearly halve the payout time. If you truly buckle down and raise your monthly contribution to 5% of the balance, you will wipe away the debt that will come from having minimum payments of 2 percent in eight years. Making larger payments might extend your income, but over time you can save thousands of dollars that can be put to greater use, accumulating capital instead of servicing debt.

You do not have a rainy-day fund

Anybody's finances might be battered by substantial healthcare, a surprise home repair, or abrupt job loss. Yet in 2019, 28 percent of Americans surveyed by Bankrate.com said they had no money set aside for emergencies at all. Just 25 percent have ample emergency savings to cover up to three months of living costs, 17 percent will cover three to five months, and only 18 percent have emergency savings for the frequently recommended six months of living expenses. You may not have to save anything at once, though you should be working on saving living costs for six months. Only set up your own separate savings account, make frequent deposits, and steadily raise the balance over time. Or try to place it on a different saving account if you need more help, which will automatically entail a transfer effort to your account and include a one-day transfer.

You have the entitlement personality

People are also stuck in purchasing items because they believe they deserve to be rewarded for minor successes or are entitled, even if they can't afford what their friends have. You become acquainted with credit card transactions or borrow money, and you are persuaded of the fact that you will later pay off what you owe. It is okay to reimburse yourself when you reach a big target, like weight loss or a new customer landing. Pay just cash and set the financial target. One example is I will buy the PlayStation 5 if I can pay off my student loan by the end of the year. Suppose you owe $20,000 in a year to buy your $500 PlayStation 5 as a good reward.

You took out too many student loans

The US owes $1.48 trillion to student loans, and payment on almost 10 percent of those loans is due at least 90 days before that, according to the Federal Reserve Bank of New York. It's not shocking that many people are trapped in debt because they have earned more student loans than they can manage. If you are either enrolled at school or your child, consider reducing the number of student loans by applying for grants and bursaries, or prevent credit by attending college, which does not require you to take out student loans. If you have a student loan and a large amount, consider getting a side job to earn extra money. I do not believe debt consolidation would be worth doing in my option, just putting off the debt for you to worry about later and taking a risk with the debt carrying on to your family if you pass away.

You cannot say NO: People end up in debt because they borrow to purchase things for their kids, family, or friends that they really can't afford—from extracurricular activities to college tuition.

Your mortgage is too big: For the Federal Reserve Bank of New York, many Americans, a mortgage may become an albatross around the neck. According to the New

York Federal Reserve Bank, these household loans constituted, on average, 68 percent of total household debt in 2019. If your mortgages are too high a charge to bear, you can need to decrease into a cheaper property, rent rather than own, or even find a staff member to help defray the cost of housing. There are a few choices if you want to be as fast as possible hypothetic-free, and you have financial flexibility. If you have an ordinary 30-year mortgage, you can raise your monthly payment to save you on interest and help you withdraw your loan early.

You live above what you get paid

It is necessary to be financially responsible for your health and financial life. "Live within your means" means that every month you spend is less or equal to the amount of money you earn every month. It is much better said than done for many people.

You do not make enough money

You can't find much more to cut when you look at your budget for extra money. You're doing without a cable now, you're not in the gym, and you're never eating away. You have a serious income problem if you have cut all that you can, and you still cannot reach ends. You will have to either find a side hustle or find a career that will pay you better. I am not talking about the people who make low income where they don't even bring in $20,000 a year and live in a high cost of living state. Everyone's situation is different, and only you can say if you just don't make enough.

You have too much liabilities

If you have a negative net worth, you have too much liability. Any amount that you owe to someone else is a liability. A debt may be short-term, as the balance on a credit card, or long-term, like a mortgage. Every liability should be used to measure your net value

- Auto loans.
- Student loans.
- Credit card balances, if not paid in full each month.
- Mortgages.

- Secured personal loans.
- Unsecured personal loans.
- Payday loans.

Chapter Five

Creating Your Life Goals

What are Life Goals?

The aspirations of life are what we want to do that help to make one of our values meaningful. They can take several different forms because they are personal goals. However, they give us a sense of purpose and make us responsible for our attempts to achieve peace and well-being—for our best lives.

Financial goals are deadlines or achievements that your money needs to cover at a given time. Your financial aim must be obvious, whether it is to create an emergency fund or to become debtless, or go on a fabulous holiday. Please be aware that purchases must not relate to your financial goals.

"We start setting goals by looking at our lifetime goals"

Starting to Set Personal Goals

You set your goals on several levels:

• You first create a 'big vision' of what you want to do with your life and describe the general objectives you want to accomplish (or for the next ten years or so).

• Then, you split them into the bigger and smaller goals you need to accomplish during your lifetime.

• Finally, you start to work on this to accomplish these objectives once you have your strategy.

Therefore, we start setting goals by looking at our lifetime goals and how to financially make them happen. We will then focus on the stuff you will do in, say, the next five years, next year, next month, next week.

Be clear about your goals

Ensure that your priorities are straightforward. Clarity can help you prevent common errors as you attempt to attain your objective. The more accurate your goal is, the more likely it is to be accomplished.

Step 1: Setting Lifetime Goals

The first step in setting your personal goals is to accept your life's goals (or at least in the future by a significant and distant age). Seeking goals for life provides you with the power to influence the other facets of making your choices. Try to set objectives in each of the following categories to provide wide, Balanced coverage of all your life's significant areas:

"Clarity can help you prevent common errors as you attempt to attain your objective"

- Career – What do you want to be doing? Do you want to be Retire or financially free?

- Financial – How much money would you like to make? What do you want your net worth to be?

- Family – Do you want kids or a family?

- Physical – Do you want to be in shape?

- Pleasure – What do you want in life to do for pleasure?

Step 2: Setting Smaller Goals

Set a five-year plan with smaller targets that you have to accomplish if you are to achieve your life plan. Develop a one-year plan, a half-month plan, and a one-month plan with increasingly smaller targets to accomplish the goals. Each must be based on the previous plan. Then build a regular To-Do list of things you can do to reach your life goals today. Earlier on, you could have smaller reading book goals and gathering knowledge on achieving your high-level goals. This will help you develop your target setting quality and realism. Last but not least, study your plans to ensure they adhere to your way of life.

Financial short-term objectives: 12-24 months

Money should be readily available and better managed on a saving account for short-term financial objectives. You may opt to make a paycheck or monthly contribution to the savings account. To produce a snowball impact, any additional sales that are not stable should be applied to the near target.

Midterm goals: 2 to 5 years

Mutual funds, CDs, and stock markets are a great place to keep money that you might not need right away. Returns are typically marginally better than the conventional economies. Mid-term financial targets could be more organized than short-term objectives and would need a little more funds. These are priorities that you will have later on.

Long-term objectives: 5+ years

The provision and definition of long-term financial aims will be important. If you don't understand why the target is important to you, it is easy to be overwhelmed with long-term objectives. That for several years you will be on the way to a longer-term target having a well-funded retirement, it's easy to lose focus on. When you recall, it may be too late for you to realize why the financial target is important for you. Since you don't necessarily need the capital, you can spend whatever money you save for a long-term financial purpose. You might consider investing in 529 plans, Stock Market, Real Estate, 401k, or Roth IRAs.

Main financial targets attributes

We need to know how much and for how long you need to save. The first step towards achieving your financial dream is to identify your financial goals and build a savings plan.

Achievable

To achieve your goals, you will need to layout action steps to make your goal attainable. I can do this by collecting more overtime for my present job or starting a side rush. Any extra income will be used to snowball financial goals.

Realistic

You will also need to create goals that are realistic based on factors like your income, time, and what you can do. It doesn't make sense to set the target of making $1 million on my bank account in 1 year, and you do not have a job. Be realistic on your goal, such as if I cut out coffee and cable and used it toward debt, I want to have 200 dollars extra pay off a month.

Time-based

Give yourself a timeline. Tell yourself; I want to have my car paid off by the end of the year or in 2 years. So, then you can budget it and figure out what needs to be done to achieve that goal. Be very specific on the date and year you want it to do not and write it down and post it everywhere so that you know this needs to be done by this time.

Chapter Six

Creating Your Financial Game Plan

So, where are you on your path to financial well-being? If that question makes you squirm, there is good news. Regardless of how much you earn, you can start building small habits each day to achieve your financial aspirations. During my research, I found there are 3 types of way people create their financial game plan. Those are the Debt Avalanche method, Debt snowball, and Starting from zero methods that I created for myself. Here I will explain what they are and which method I had picked to set myself up for the future. Both of these strategies are nearly similar in that they both require you to make minimum payments on all your loans, with one emphasis on debt.

With either method, you will spend every extra dollar you can find until the focus debt is paid off. Once it is, then the next debt in line becomes your new focus debt. You're going to have more and more money to give to the debt you are targeting as you max out your loans and your minimum payments. The only difference between snowball and avalanche is your loan payment.

The Debt Snowball Method

You first pay the lowest balance to the greatest debt using the debt snowball approach, regardless of the interest rate. I believe this idea works great for 90% of people because it helps to build up a habit and give you short-term rewards, which will help motivate you. The reason for this is often, People have a lot of small debts, and when all of these bills come in, it can be overwhelming. That tends to defer people to try to work on their debt because of the overwhelming pressure.

It all just too overwhelming when it seems like you, everyone, and their mom is knocking on your door for 10, 20, and 100 dollars at the end of the month. When you pay your debt smallest to largest balance, you start to clear those little debts extremely quickly. Depending on your situation you might be in.

When you see results easily, the feeling is overwhelming, and you start thinking for yourself that you can, especially if you work all these extra hours or start a side rush.

Debt Pros

• This is a working procedure. Thousands pay millions of dollars in this form (just check out all the Dave Ramsey debt-free screams).

• All the debit balances can be seen.

• Some quick psychological benefits can be made by first repaying your smallest debt.

• Your snowball should be high until you hit your biggest debt.

Debt Ball Benefits

There is only one big con of the process of the debt snowball. It ignores interest rates and thus may not be the correct approach mathematically.

The Debt Avalanche Method

In the debt avalanche method, you pay your debts from highest interest rate to lowest interest rate, regardless of balance. I do not recommend this method just for anyone. A normal person that in debt has bad spending habits or still does not understand how to handle money. The only people a recommend this method is a financial nerd.

"Saving money on interest means you will pay your debts off more quickly"

People who understand finances and have full control of their money just ran into a few bad situations of trying to help a family member out, their partner bringing in debt, and just had disaster events happen to them financially.

Mathematically this makes the most sense. You will pay less in interest if you tackle your debts in this order. Saving money on interest means you will pay your debts off more quickly. Isn't the whole point of getting out of debt to do it as quickly as possible? When you first take on the highest interest rate, you get the hardest fight. Normally this route, you can pay off debt faster and save more money from debt, but if you are not motivated, you will quickly spiral out of control.

Pros of the Debt Avalanche

• It is mathematically optimal.

• All of your loan balances can be seen.

• This approach is going to succeed.

• You are gaining an avalanche momentum as you pay off your debts.

Avalanche's Debt Poor

As with the debt snowball, I guess there's only one big con. Your highest interest-rate debt is your largest equilibrium debt. If so, it will take a while to gain momentum. I fear that many will give up because some little ones won't pay off the psychological benefit.

Starting from Zero method step

This is the method that I created for my use and that I have used to help others. It used the best of both worlds. Using all the knowledge I learned and knowing my mindset; I created this method. Starting from the Zero method is exactly what the name says you need to sit down and know exactly how much money you need to live off.

Step 1: Zero

What is your minimal expense to live off? This will help determine if you have a spending problem or an income problem.

Step 2: Attack

Write down all your balance for everything. Categorize what a need and what is not. I am the same on the snowball method to pay all small debt lower than $2,000 of the first list them from lowest to highest.

Step 3: Calculation

Here is where it defers from the snowball method because now I focus on saving money. I now calculate all the rest of my debt, excluding the mortgage, and put them from highest interest rate to the lowest and pay it off in that order. I will also start to invest a little sum of money in understanding how to build up my net worth. You do not start investing until your net worth is in the positive.

I believe this method will work for people who get serious about paying off their debt. The key to this method and is a success is you build up your habit of attacking your debt, and during the process, you start to think about an investment, which will be discussed in chapter 10.

The most important thing here is to pay off your debts. If you have a preference to use one method over the other, go for it!

By combining the two, you will get the pros of both methods, and with larger balance debts, interest does matter.

Chapter Seven

Creating My Personal Wealth

Now that you have the goals, knowledge of the rule of money and the how you are going to get out of debt. You will now have to start creating your future. Nobody cares more than you about your finances, so you must have a financial plan for yourself. A sound financial plan will help you save money, deliver what you want, and achieve long term objectives such as saving money for college and pension.

This probably will not come as a surprise, but everyone's financial plan looks different. We all crave financial freedom and wealth creation. It is a great deal to decide to set out on the path to financial freedom! It's a fresh start with your money, and you go to something that might change your life for the better.

These are the step that I took to help build my family generation wealth. These steps have applied all the knowledge you have read in this book so far so apply them to create your method. This method is not for everyone, and you should speak with a financial advisor to find what best fits yours or make an educated decision on exactly what method works best for you in your situation. This method is one I created after researching the best possible way mentally, physically, and relationship for everyone around you. I called this method the Zero method.

Step 1: Find your expenses

Finding what you need to just keep your standard of living going. This step is to look at your last 3-month expense report before going on to the next step. The reason we are doing this is to see what your financial mindset and spending habit are. Use this chance to see what rules of money and financial secret you are doing well and failing at. This is a great chance to sit down and humble oneself and understand that you need help.

Make out a Calculated Cost Sheet of all expenses for each month, fixed expenses such as rent, electricity, etc., first, followed by food, gasoline, clothing, and other non-fixed expenses. Average everything out for the past three months, and you will have an estimate for the monthly expenses, and then multiply by three. The estimate will be approximate, but not exact, since expenses vary, and there could be unforeseen bills that crop up, such as car breakdowns, etc.

This step can take from a few days to a month to compile all your debit and expense into one form and to get it to organize with your partner. Expect a lot of arguing and resentment if you are doing this with your partner. This will be one of the biggest fights in your life with your partner going over this expense report. This should be a conversation explain that this is the pass there is nothing we can do about it now, but what can we do to move forward to fix this situation.

Step 2: Become a Budget Master

I have broken this into two steps as mentally; it takes weeks or months to work with your partner or to do this solo, depending on your relationship status. This step will take constant modification to get this step down perfectly until you can find how you want to. Earlier in the book, I mentioned what method I used to get out of debt, yours will be determined by you. You can first measure your sales to build a budget.

Step a: Add up your fixed monthly income

List all your income in your budgeting tool, whether that is at the top of a page or in an excel spreadsheet. This step is important. Do not leave anything out. Include all sources of income.

It's just the money they take from their salaries for many people. Yet you want to include all of your money on your budget if you are a company owner or have extra revenue from a side rush. Try the best you can to predict your monthly income this month. Take the average of the last three months of income and use it as your income if your income is incompatible.

Step b: Go back to the expense report and compare it to your income.

This step is one of the most important steps in the whole Zero Method. Determine how aggressive you will be to get out of debt or how you will live with debt. This step is where you sit down with your partner or decided for yourself how you want to live your life.

Determine if you are going to get out of debt in 1 month or ten years. This is where everyone plans to defer. My plan is to out of debt in a reasonable amount of time with also starting to build up wealth at the same time. This is where you decided if you need to get a better career, job, 2nd job, work overtime, or create a side hustle.

Building on the above example, your expenses now will appear like these;

Expenses/Budget

Rent: $1,000

Electric: $25

Gas: $20

Groceries: $350

Emergency fund savings: $300

Car Savings: $200

Debt repayment: $400

Dining out: $75

Hair and Beauty: $50

Other: $150

Step 3: Determine how you are going to get out of debt.

Now you know exactly how much you are in debt, you can choose how you want to get out of debt from one of the methods in this book. I had used the zero method. This one helps me take advantage of some of the tax loophole and employee match so that I did not miss my opportunity for compound interest. This financial make the most sense for anyone younger and have time on their hand. These are the step used to get out of debt and build up wealth.

Zero to Million Method

Step 1: Emergency fund

Save one month of the bare minimum expenses you need to survive. This can be any amount of money that you need to pay for rent, utility, and food. You need to save one month just in case you get fire or needing it for another emergency, so you have time to get another job:

Example:

Rent: 1000

Utility: 200

Food: 200

Total: 1400

This step should be done ASAP to save this amount of money.

Step 2: Pay off all the low debt under 2 thousand dollars lowest to highest

Stop all forms of investing and focus on having this done within six months to 1 year. Picking up over time, 2nd job, or side hustle doesn't matter; you are getting out of debt. There only a few ways to speed this method up to make more money or spend less money. What I did was did a mixture. I didn't want to give up my fishing habit, which is pretty pricy, but I did lower my expense for it to a reasonable amount and cut everything else out that didn't have much use like coffee, going out to eat was reduce to 100 from 300 a month, cheaper insurance, cheaper cellphone plan, etc.

"Save one month of the bare minimum expenses you need to survive"

Step 3: Determine your net worth

This step is a simple asset- liability= net worth.

Calculating your net worth requires you to take an inventory of what you own, as well as your outstanding debt. And when we say own, we include assets that you may still be paying for, such as a car or a house. If you are in negative net worth, you still must focus on paying off debt until you can get back into the positive before moving to step 4. Go back to step one and pick your lowest owe debt, and keep it up until you see the number go from red to black in your book.

Step 4: Building your saving muscle

This is where you slowly start putting away for retirement or investing. You now take your original salary before your overtime, 2nd job, side hustle, or any other method and take 5% of that income after taxes of the overall. In this step, you finish paying off all your debit—highest interest rate to lowest excluding your mortgage.

Example:

Salary at the primary job: $50,000

Side Income: $20,000

Total income: $70,000

Take-home pay after taxes: $63,179

Taxes paid: $70,000- $63,179= $6,821

Salary base to use the %5: $50,000-$6,821=$43,179

How much to invest: $2,158.95 a year or $179.91 a month

Your situation:

Salary at the primary job: $

Side Income: $

Total income: $

Take home pay after taxes: X .91 = taxes paid

Salary base to use the %5: -$=$

How much to invest: $ a year or $a month

We start investing because overall, the $179.91 you are passing up on employee match. If your employee match 3% of your salary at $50,000 that, is $1,500 a year of free money you are passing up. In the very first year, without any knowledge of what to invest, you have already double your money on the first $1,500—anything over the match you will put into the Roth IRA, which is tax-free.

Where to invest the money:

1. Match Employee Retirement Roth
2. Match Employee Retirement
3. Roth IRA
4. Health Saving Plan

The IRA is a tax-favored investment mechanism that people use to earmark retirement savings accounts. Multiple forms of IRAs exist.

- Traditional IRAs
- Roth IRAs
- SEP IRAs
- SIMPLE IRAs

Types of IRAs

Traditional IRA

In most cases, tax-deductibility extends to conventional IRAs. If anyone puts $5,000 in an IRA, that person's taxable income will decrease by the donation amount. But withdrawals are taxed at the normal tax rate when the person is withdrawing money from the account during retirement.

Roth IRA

Roth IRAs are not tax-exempt, but they are tax-free in terms of eligible distributions. You contribute with post-tax dollars to a Roth IRA, but you have no investment gain tax. When you retire, without income tax on your withdrawals, you will withdraw from the account. There are no RMDs for Roth IRAs, too. You don't have to take the money off your account if you don't need it. If you have qualifying earned income, you can still apply to Roth IRA no matter how old you are.

SEP IRA

The SEP IRAs can be set up by self-employed people, including independent contractors, self-employed people, and small-scale business owners. The SEP acronym is a 'Simplified Pension for Employees'. A SEP IRA adheres to the same financial laws as a standard IRA for withdrawals.

SIMPLE IRA

The Easy IRA is also for SMEs and individuals who work for themselves. The Basic abbreviation is the "savings incentive match plan for employees". The same fiscal principles apply to withdrawals as the standard IRA. Unlike SEP IRAs, SIMPLE IRAs allow workers to pay contributions, and the employer has to make payments. Both tax contributions are deductible, which may contribute to a lower tax base for the corporation or employee.

Health Savings Account (HSA)

A sort of savings account that allows for eligible medical expenses to pay money on a pre-tax basis. You will reduce the total healthcare costs by using untaxed dollars on your HSA account to cover deductibles, copayments, coinsurance, and other expenses. Usually, HSA funds cannot be used for paying premiums.

Key Notes:

- Pay off High Interest to Low-Interest debt.
- Start saving for retirement help give you motivation because you get to see the light at the end of the tunnel.
- Start Building your investment muscle and take advantage of employee match.

Step 5: Emergency fund

Now, this step is simple. You have all your debt paid off, you start to invest a little amount of money, but your rainy-day fund is too small; if a major emergency comes up, you will go back in step so to prevent this from happening. I recommend you have at the minimum three months of expense in your account for a stable job and six months for an unstable income job. What type of account you put it in doesn't matter; as long as you can get your funds in 1 day in your hand is all that matters.

"Start focusing on investing 15% of your total salary into a different retirement account"

Keynote:

- Still have your 2nd job.

- Treat this like debit put the money into a saving account.

- Prevent you from falling into debt again

Step 6: Save for a house/ Pay for your house

Now that all your debt is paid off, you can now start focusing on investing 15% of your total salary into a different retirement account. This is time you can decide if you want to keep your extra income. I recommend keeping the side income long enough that you can save 20% down on a house that is no more than 1/3 of your monthly take home. What type of loan should you get depend on your situation you want to put yourself in. Should it be a 5, 10, 15, 30-year loan?

I believe you should enjoy your money and not make your life revolve around becoming a millionaire or become super-wealthy. What the point of having a million-dollar and you die tomorrow. I bought my house at a 30-year fixed rate. Some financial advisors were telling me you are messing up your life; you should never do a 30-year fix rate, should do a 10-year or 15-year so you can have your house paid off faster.

Yes, I believed you should pay off your house in 10-years so I can go into complete retirement debit free. But here is my argument what happens if I do not make it to retirement, and I was so focused on paying for this house with the extra income that I did not get to enjoy my money.

In this Step:

- 15% into a retirement account (Employee match, Roth and Health Saving Plan)
- 15% into Fun money start enjoying your money
- 20% Investment whatever avenue you want to take (Rental, Mutual fund, stock market, etc.)
- 50% on to paying off your house early

If you do not have a house, then this is where you save for a down payment depending on where you can take you a few months or a few years. Instead of investing 20% on an investment, you will now put 70% on to saving for a house.

Step 7: Enjoy being debit free.

You've finished building your emergency fund, started your retirement, and began investing. Do not forget to use your new found financial freedom to enjoy your life.

Maybe it is time to plan your dream vacation, get the thing you away wanted, or help others. This is all on you now. My biggest advice here is don't go back in to debit for liabilities and focus on enjoying your money.

Now that you are out of debt, you are in a position now to do the things you enjoy the most. Take advantage of it. You worked hard to get here.

Chapter Eight

Finding Extra Income

How to Develop a Successful Side Hustle

Here are some helpful hints on finding a successful side hustle.

Make a list of what you are interested in

You need to enjoy what you are doing as a side hustle so that you don't get burned out. If you have a workday, it takes a lot of energy and determination to make this work stick. It is done at your own time and outside working hours. You're just going to be motivated by what you love. Brainstorms side invites you to ideas about the best ways to start or see how you can turn a hobby into a company based on your interests and abilities.

Decide early if you're going to spend capital

The side hustle does not cost too much money, but it may need some investment early for items like hosting, branding, and software; you can opt to advertise to find the first clients. Regardless of the strategy for development and expansion, you have to be conscious of the spending before it occurs.

Ensure that there is no interest in conflicts

It is not a good idea to proceed if you have a day work or relationships that might lead to a conflict of interest with your side-effort. Often you should try another thing or cover your idea so that you don't end up doing something you regret. A side rush could lead to costly lessons learned by a conflict of interest.

Plan your side hustle, period

Side chaos takes time off your every day schedule, so make sure everything goes well. You cannot set up your website, program your content, and forget everything until next month. Set time off regularly in your calendar for your hustle and set actionable targets to ensure that what you do is worthwhile.

Do not forget your day jobs. Don't forget!

If you set aside business when you still have a day's job, remember to place 100% of your focus on your day's work. You may have a side hustle but depend on your check to cover your day's work bills. Don't try to bring your work and your daytime hustle into effect within 9 to 5 hours, as this is a catastrophe formula. The generation and balance of extra money are one of the most successful debt reduction strategies. That is because it allows you to get out of debt faster and pay less interest without eating into your monthly budget.

Selling items online

You're looking for a way to collect some quick cash if you're low on cash or you have to have extra money to go into your debt. It's cool to sell items that you do not have or use to raise money for stuff you want to do, but you don't have the money for in your budget. You must look for the best way to sell your goods at the best price and choose the place to sell your items.

Below is one of the ways you can find an extra item to sell for free.

Garbage - That is the right garbage. You can drive around on trash day or find a dumpster to dive in and resell it on eBay. I found all types of good on the side of the road that was worth 100 dollars. People throw things that are worth value and can bring you $1,000 a month with just a very minimal amount of work. For craft projects, empty toilet paper and paper towel tubes are required. Boxes of shoes and jewelry that are empty sales as well as birch boxes and card boxes of baseball. Some people wish to buy old sweeper and remote sweeper bits. Check to see if you can sell it online before throwing it out. It doesn't hurt to drive around and google what thing is worth before taking it home to sell. There are other avenues to find a thing to make money, but it will not be cover in this book as this about how to your financial knowledge and how to build wealth and not how to create an online sale company.

Gain more hours

One of the best ways to earn more money is by working more. If you have a job every hour, let your boss and colleagues know you can cover additional shifts. If required, you can also willingly work overtime, for example, if your team is under-personalized or especially busy.

Get a second job

If you are an employee or cannot get extra hours at work, consider taking a second job to raise additional income. Tipping-based employment may be especially profitable such as waiting, bartending, or supplying food. Many distributors often employ seasonal staff for their most busy periods of the year.

Providing independent or contract services

Furthermore, skilled employees and practitioners will also do more during their hours if they can use their know-how to ask for higher wages. If you earn more with every hour you work, you will spend even more money on debt. From marketing and web creation to home refurbishment, you can offer your services as a free-standing contractor or contractor. You can then use your off-hours to make some serious extra cash.

Teach others an ability

Another way to learn your specific skills is to teach people a course, a class, or individual lessons. You will produce a few hundred dollars a month to make additional debt payments with just a few hours of instruction per week. You can teach private lessons, for example, if you can play or sing a musical instrument. Workers who lead a fitness class may find employment or work as an individual trainer.

Services of care

Even to make some additional income to help pay your mortgage, you can offer care services. People are away looking for a babysitter and pet sitter. There is plenty of online services that can assist you in finding a gig.

Chapter Nine

How To Invest Money

The most effective way to build wealth over time is to invest your capital. The general difference between how you invest your money and how I set my investment to develop large amounts of money will be spelled out if you're new to investing. You would need a basic understanding of how this works before you put your hard-earned money in an investment fund. Some of the safest ways to spend capital are as follows:

Retirement Account and Investment Account

Stock Market

Dividend Stock

Dividend stocks can provide both stable income and long-term growth opportunities for investors. However, all the dividend stocks are not great investments, and many investors are not sure how to look.

"The most effective way to build wealth over time is to invest your capital"

Stocks

Investments in the potential success of a business are termed stock. You benefit from them when you invest in an inventory of a business.

Bonds

Much as borrowing money for most citizens is part of life, corporations and communities often borrow money through bonds.

Index Funds

A market index is tracked by this popular investment vehicle and can help balance your portfolio.

ETFs

Learn about ETFs or exchange-traded funds that trade like stocks. However, there is no correct way to invest your money. Whichever way works best for you is the best way to invest capital. You'll want to consider to find that out:

- Risk tolerance
- The fund that is available to invest
- Passive or Active

Risk Tolerance

Not all investments will away payout or become successful. Every investor has its risk level, but the higher the risk is also connected to returns. It is important to find a balance between maximizing your cash returns and seeking a degree of risk that you are comfortable with. For example, bonds deliver extremely low-risk, stable returns, and generate a relatively low return of about 2-3%. In comparison, stock yields vary considerably according to industry and timelines, but on average, the entire stock market returns about 12% each year.

The fund that is available to invest

You will think that you need a large amount to start a portfolio, but you can start investing by 10$. We also have fantastic $1,000 investment ideas. The money with which you start is not the most important thing. How long can you invest your capital? A big move forward is to build an emergency fund before investing. This is cash in a form available for fast withdrawal. Any investment, whether securities, reciprocal funds, or land, is at risk, and you will never have to divest (or sell) these assets in a time of need. Your safety net is the emergency fund for this reason. The truth is, any time you have a flat tyre or an unexpected expense, you just don't want to have to sell your savings.

Passive or Active

When it comes to financing; aggressive investment and passive investment, the investment world has two main camps. Both styles have it for the long term and are not only looking for short-term gains. You can, however, be chosen by your lifestyle, budget, risk tolerance, and interests. Active investing means you take time to research your investments and develop and manage your portfolio. You are planning to be an active investor if you plan to buy and sell individual stocks from an online broker. You need three things to succeed in being an active investor.

<u>Time</u>: Successful investment demands a great deal of homework. You will need to investigate investment opportunities, perform fundamental analyses, and keep up with your investment after buying it.

Knowledge: If you do not know how to analyze and research investments properly, you will not gain at any time in the world. You should know the basic principles for evaluating stocks, at least before investing in stocks. At least before you invest in stocks, you should know the fundamentals about how to evaluate stocks.

Desire: Sometimes, people don't want to commit for hours. And as passive investing has traditionally created strong profits, the strategy is unfounded. Active investment is capable of higher returns, but you need to spend time doing it right in the long term, and the commitment needed is much smaller.

Passive investing

- More simplicity, more stability, more predictability
- Not actively managing
- Moderate returns
- Tax advantages

Active investing

- More work, more risk, the more potential reward
- You do the investing yourself (or through a portfolio manager)
- Lots of research
- Potential for huge, life-changing return income

Real estate

You can choose hundreds of ways to invest in real estate. The good thing is, no one direction is better than the others. When done right. So, we'll look at how to invest in real estate using various approaches instead of telling which one is the best.

Real estate investment trusts (REITs)

Real estate investment trusts are organizations where investors pool their money to invest in a portfolio of assets that are not individually available. REITs make money from the lease, rental, or sale of owned assets. Since trusts are formed, there are rules about what form of assets they own and how capital can be returned through dividends to shareholders. Many REITs specialize in a specific category of an asset, such as homes, mortgages, healthcare, or infrastructure. Some of its features includes:

- Low-cost point of entry
- It is good for investors looking for value for their money and a rise in dividends
- It is perfectly kept in tax-favored accounts.
- Recurrent cash, capital increase, and multiple tax benefits
- Power to use equity to buy a property and raise return rates.
- Choice of short or long term rentals
- It takes longer and more money, but you can make a big difference.
- Houses to flip
- Return rates are high.
- Investing inland
- Less expensive than buying developed property
- Requires a lot of foresight
- Can sell a lot at a time

Starting A Business

Starting a successful business doesn't need to require a huge investment. With a great business idea and the right tools, you can start a business without investing much money or even acquiring inventory. The type of business is all determined by you and what you believed that be successful. This investment has the biggest risk with the highest reward.

The Investment Strategy I used

How I invested my money is overly aggressive compared to your traditional method. Due to my age, I had more time on my hand to recover from my financial mistake. I took the non-traditional route and started a business with almost no cost. The amount of time I took to start my business to start bringing in an actual income was about four years and a ton and ton of money reinvesting back into the company. Now that business is self-ran and brings in a large amount of income; it was risky and incredibly stressful.

The 2nd way I am investing is that I am currently investing in a company 401k, Roth IRA, and an HSA account. I did not stop investing in my longer-term goal; while I was building my company, I did not want to ruin my future to chase after a dream. That makes up about 15% of my income.

The 3rd way I am investing is by putting away 15% into dividend stock, mutual funds, and index in my investment account.

The final way I invest is into long term rental property. I do only turnkey rental property. I do not do a flip house or look for a house to fix up and rent out the house because I do not have much time on my hand to do so.

Is my method of investing for my future correct? Maybe, but it's my financial journey and not yours.

Chapter Ten

Money Scammers And Protecting Your Money

There are scammers looking to trick you out of your money. They can take your life savings and put you in a poor house. Artists and disreputable corporations can do or say what they want to get but you must be alert. Sometimes, after you wired money or give your personal information out on the phone, you become screwed. There is no getting that money back or that information; you will have to go and get all your information change just so that they stop taking your money. If you are searching for them, like most scams, there are warning signs. Don't trust anyone to question everything. You can create a fake website overnight with great reviews, fake numbers, and copy logo in the digital age. Before you give any information out, you need to do some research and have some common knowledge. No company should just call you and ask for your social security, birthdate, and other personal information. Think about it and check it before you reply. You could not risk thousands of dollars or give away very personal details by calling or searching for a quick web search. I even hang up and google search phone number and found that it said that number is a scam.

"There are scammers looking to trick you out of your money"

Double your investment is a scam. If you get an email, phone call, someone tells you in person tthat if you give me $1,000 I can double your money, if it sounds too good, then it is a scam. Just do not do it. Use a credit card for online transactions. Credit cards have greater protection against theft than debit cards – different federal laws regulate credit cards. You can challenge an illegal fee with the credit card, and you must take the bill off during inspection by the credit card company. For a debit card, this is not always the case. Even if the products haven't arrived or faulty, and the business won't help you, you can challenge a credit card fee. Don't let someone try to rush into making a transaction; take your time. The purchase or purchase strategy is designed to discourage you from shopping in contrast. Guard your personal information, fraudsters use a variety of tricks to get you to divulge account numbers and passwords. They send fake emails designed to look like it's from your bank and make calls pretending to be with your credit card company. They will threaten you with a common theme, for con artists will say that they will send you to jail if you don't do what they tell you or get fired if you don't do this. Hang up the phone and call the police station if you are worried that you are going to get arrested for something as they have to be a warrant for your arrest first.

Protecting your Asset

There are many ways you can protect your assets. The best way to figure out how to protect your assets is to contact a law firm and an accountant so that you can find the best way legally to protect your assets. Also, after reach a certain significant amount of wealth, you will need to get Personal liability insurance.

Who Needs Personal Liability Insurance?

You can take personal liability insurance into account as soon as you live on your own and are liable for your actions. The renters, landlords, and condo policy require the expense of basic personal liability insurance, amounting to only a few dollars a month. And if you don't think you have anything to lose right now if you are responsible for personal injuries or damages to property, your potential assets are at risk too. You cannot risk current assets such as stocks, apartments, and other properties; you also should note the probability of garnishing future income such as salaries or impacting future assets when there are no existing assets!

Moreover, how are you falsely convicted and compelled to stand trial, even if the claim is false? The coverage of obligations will fund defense expenses and provide legal advice. Everyone knows, attorneys and lawyers can cost you a lot, and it can cost you all to engage in a case. Insurance for personal responsibility covers you in three ways:

Present and potential assets are covered by personal responsibility. You will have coverage for your protection if an action is taken against you, irrespective of whether it is your fault or not, through your home insurance, condo insurance, or renter insurance. It helps keep you from being able to pay legal defense charges. Personal responsibility may cover your claims, including physical injuries to others, on or caused by you as a result of an accident.

The personal duty also covers you and your family members around the world for work at and off the premises. This includes accidents and even things that might happen because of your fault. This is just a general list of what they cover, and you will have to read your contract at the time of signing to see what you are cover for. People are very sued happy in the day and age so protect yourself from them from taking everything you own.

Conclusion

If you become one of the lucky few, who become successful from reading this book and follow the rules of money and getting out of debt, you are going to also need to learn how to enjoy your money. After all those years of grinding away to save this wealth, you got to have fun with it too. Here are someways to enjoy your money;

- Buy experiences rather than material goods.
- Taking family trips or experience traveling will last you forever.
- It is okay to buy things if they can lead to pleasurable experiences.
- Spend money to help others.
- Donate to people in need. Help a person that can't afford a cancer treatment on their children.
- Buy yourself small treats.
- Buying yourself a game system or a shorter trip to enjoy the weekend.
- If you are going for a day out, do not calculate how much you could have earned if you had worked instead.
- Go out one day and just spend some money on the thing you want without looking at the number. Just do not go too crazy.
- Remember that not spending can be satisfying too.
- Spend it on a hobbies.
- Spend it on the education or training you always wanted.

You just read on how to become financially wealthy and how you should allow your money mindset to be stuck as a child. Don't let the money be too big for you to handle, but how you should become its master and enjoy the reward of having money work for you. Now, what is stopping you from becoming wealthy? Everyone has excuses to become the person with the answer.